What I Always Meant to Say

A Father's Letters to His Daughters

Gregory Thomas Walker

Dedication

This book is dedicated to my wonderful daughters, Gaelyn and Erryn.

Table of Contents

INTRODUCTION

Train up a child in the way he should go, and when he is old, he will not depart from it.

- Proverbs 22:6

Where you sit when you are old shows where you stood in youth

– African proverb

After 19-plus years of fatherhood of two wonderful and amazing daughters, I realized that, despite my best intentions, we had not consistently communicated well. Or, I should say, that I had not consistently communicated well. While throughout your upbringing, we've had many conversations, discussions, lectures, arguments and disputes, I realized suddenly that at the ages of 19 and 15, you had probably heard more things from me that you may not have needed to hear, and less of the things you really should have heard. To be honest, it gave me a sense of great inadequacy as a parent. I realized that too often I may have gotten caught up in the mundane, trivial, urgent or heated issues of the day, and the ultimate consequence was that I didn't convey to you some things of more lasting importance.

I do not doubt that you know that I love you both dearly and that your happiness and well-being (along with that of your mother) have been my primary motivation and goal in life. However, I feel that many things I've wanted to pass along to you to help prepare you for adulthood, I've left unsaid. I accept the responsibility for this. Sometimes these topics were complex for me to discuss with you, or the timing wasn't right, or I was concerned you'd "tune me out." Yet, as I noted above, I felt I had not done my job as your father if I left that feeling unaddressed.

I struggled for a couple of years with what to do about this situation. After considering several options and discussing it with your mother, I decided to do it as a book of letters to you. Hopefully, you will find this less boring and intrusive than having a "father-daughter talk," and more valuable and meaningful. Anyway, I think I'm better at communicating in writing than verbally. So, I trust this will work out best for all of us. However, I am always willing to discuss anything I write with you at any time. Maybe this will give us even more to talk about. So, here goes....

ALWAYS REMEMBER THAT YOU ARE LOVED

As the father has loved me, so have I loved you; abide in my love.

- John 15:9

Dear Gaelyn and Erryn,

As I write my first letter in this book to you, this is where I have to start. I love you both more than you'll ever know. It is ocean deep and sky high. My love is unconditional, irrevocable, and everlasting. Your mother certainly loves you just as much, but no one on earth loves you more than I do.

I've tried to make it a point to say I love you every day we've been together. You've heard it from the womb to right now. And I meant it every time I've said it. I've done that (and will continue to do it as long as I live) for two reasons.

The first is because it's true. You both mean the world to me. You have been the joy of my life since your birth. I've appreciated being your father immensely, and I am extremely proud of you both. I thank God daily for you, and I pray that he blesses you as richly as you've been a blessing to me.

The second reason is that I never want you to question whether you are loved. Regardless of what you do, where you go, what you experience, whom you choose as a companion (or if you never choose one), you have my love. I may not always agree with what you do, but that will never affect how I feel about you two.

Whatever challenges, opportunities, successes, disappointments, stresses, or strains you experience throughout life, always know this love is there for you.

Love always,

Dad

FAITH MATTERS

For we walk by faith, not by sight.

- 2 Corinthians 5:7

God is our neighbor when our brother is absent.

– African Proverb

Dear Gaelyn and Erryn,

While we've not had many discussions on faith considerations, I want to make sure that I cover this topic up front as well. I have several points to make here, and I'll try not to be too long-winded. However, I feel very strongly about this, please forgive me if I run on a bit.

As you know, you've both been raised in a church-going household. To her credit, your mother (Sharon) has made it absolutely necessary that we be in church every Sunday and that you all have some direct involvement in church related activity. As you may recall, I was moved to tears during both of your baptisms (in addition to your christenings) because of my overflowing joy in your decision to accept Jesus Christ as your Lord and Savior. Our Sunday ritual of attending services as a family was always a joy to me (whether I stayed awake through the sermon or not) because I appreciated the significance of us all being together. And, I believed in the long run that the habit of being in church on Sunday and connecting to a spiritual community would be of lasting benefit to you both.

I'm glad to see that this has indeed played out in your lives, as you've continued to attend church whether at home, away at school, or living on your own. In my judgment, being part of a community of believers is very important. Having attended many different churches in different cities during my life, I've found the access to a place where my faith is appreciated, nourished, and fortified to be significantly beneficial. Whether attending Sunday services or just sitting in an empty sanctuary for a spell during the week, the church has served as a touchstone for me, helping me to sort through a variety of personal, professional and social issues, opening my heart to God in prayer, providing a comforting environment where I could be quiet and listen to God speaking to me (sometimes from the words of a minister, a song from the choir, a meaningful comment from a fellow worshiper, or from the small voice that speaks to us from inside our heart or conscience). I hope and pray that you, too, will find the church to be a similar source of comfort and renewal, reinforcing you in every way to deal with life's challenges.

Speaking of prayer, I hope you both have learned to appreciate the value and power of prayer. I am a big believer in this. There is nothing too great or too small to pray about. I believe prayer should be as much a part of your daily routine as breathing or eating. It doesn't have to be long or full of flowery phrases. It just needs to be honest and sincere. Prayer and Bible reading are the keys to developing a relationship with God. The scriptures provide you with an understanding of God based upon the statutes provided, the relationships others have had with Him, and through the teachings of Jesus and his disciples.

However, it's through prayer that you develop your personal connection. This is your conversation with God, your opportunity to express yourself and to open yourself to His response. Just as you would with us or your friends, you need to dialogue with God to establish and cement your personal relationship with the Almighty. Believe me, prayer is a powerful resource to utilize during both the good times and the bad times in life. I try to start every day with a prayer, and at minimum, make it a point just to say "Thank you, God" at some point during the day. My desire and request are that you make time for prayer and use it to build your relationship with God.

Third, I believe in reading the Bible and, most importantly, learning some scriptures. As Christians, the Bible is our resource for understanding our faith. It provides profound teachings on God's love and grace, His expectations for us, his willingness to forgive and accept us, and his commitment to be with us through life's trials and challenges. It amazes me how often I've met Christians who profess their belief and faith, but who have no real foundation for their beliefs from an understanding of the Bible. I honestly believe that this is the biggest problem in Christianity, the ignorance of the Bible itself. So many people rely solely on the interpretation (or misinterpretation) of the scriptures by others (be they clergy or non-clergy), that they fail to develop their understanding by reading the Bible themselves. Don't fall into that trap. Reinforce and enhance your faith by understanding what you believe based on knowledge of the scriptures. I've read the Bible cover to cover twice and, while not as dedicated as your mother in participating in Bible study groups, I make time to read a passage of scripture nearly every day (from my Daily Word, my Bible, or even from an online scripture reading website). If you come across or encounter something you don't understand or have an issue with, feel free to discuss it with us, a minister, another Christian, or just pray for insight ("Knock, and the door will be opened."). Also, commit some verses to memory, particularly ones that are meaningful to you, that encourage, instill confidence, and provide reassurance. I've found these to be especially useful for me when I'm anxious, uncertain, fearful, frustrated, or discouraged. Be reminded that the power that is in you is greater than that in the world.

There is a minister Sharon and I used to watch on TV (Rev. Dr. Fredrick C. K. Price). The theme of his TV ministry was Ever-Increasing Faith, and his program had a theme song called Evidence. The refrain for the song went: "Evidence! Evidence! Does your life show enough evidence? Evidence! Evidence! Could they put you away?" From the first time I heard it, I always thought that was a great consideration for a Christian. Does the way you live your life show evidence of your belief and faith? We're all imperfect, but do you demonstrate enough of what you believe that you could be convicted of being a Christian? We're not all called to be evangelists, Sunday school teachers, deacons, or choir members. But, we can all have a "church home," we can all pray, and we can all read our Bibles. If you do those things and live out your beliefs, that's all the evidence you'll need.

Love always,

Dad

BE TRUE TO YOU

The purpose in a man's mind is like deep water, but a man of understanding will draw it out.

- Proverbs 20:5

Wherever a man goes to dwell, his character goes with him.

– African proverb

Dear Gaelyn and Erryn,

In Shakespeare's Hamlet, Polonius advises his son Laertes, "To thine own self be true." I think this is one of the best pieces of advice any parent can give their child. So, I'd like to extend this same advice to you, with a little spin of my own. I think there are several aspects of being true to yourself, and my thoughts on those aspects are covered below.

First, you need to spend some time getting to understand who you are. For most of your life, you've had your parents guiding and directing your personal development. Now that you are adults, you need to assess for yourself what makes you who you are. What are your beliefs, values, and principles? How do you define yourself? What matters most to you, and what are your priorities?

What type of person do you want to be, and what are the qualities you want to exhibit? What are your likes and dislikes? What makes you happy or unhappy? These are the types of questions you should ask yourself, and answer honestly. There are no wrong answers to these questions when you're being honest with yourself because they are all about you. No one else can answer them for you, and only you can decide what the answers are. I recommend that you make some time to have a "heart to heart" talk with yourself. Write these questions down and thoughtfully write out your responses. Then, come back a few days later, look at what you wrote, and see if you still agree with it. Reflect on these answers and think about what the implications of your answers mean. Don't be surprised if you find that you can't answer some of the questions. That's OK. In fact, it could take you weeks or months to get to a final answer (sometimes, even years), but the time and effort are worth it. I can testify that this exercise is one of the best things I've ever done, and it's influenced every major decision I've made in my adult life (and many of the minor ones, too).

Once you've defined yourself (or at least started the process), the next step is to assess the direction your life is taking and whether it is consistent with who you are (or want to be). I think a lot of the stress that people have in life is, in large measure, a reflection of the conflict between how they perceive themselves (or wish to be perceived) and the reality of how they're living. The more you can live a life that reflects who you are, the more contentment you will find in your daily living. I think that is when your life is in balance. You are being yourself and living your life. When they are out of balance (doing a job you dislike, being in a relationship that compromises or conflicts with your beliefs and values, getting into habits that make you feel bad about yourself, living somewhere that you dislike), it is virtually impossible to feel good about yourself and to be the person you want to be. When left unresolved, these situations can have a damaging effect on your psyche, personality, relationships, performance, and even your health. I contend that people who are negative, bitter, cynical, confrontational, and just generally difficult to be around are casualties of this imbalance in their lives. While I believe it is possible for people to change these attitudes, I've rarely seen it happen. So, it's best to avoid allowing yourself to get to that point. I can attest that the major changes I've made in my life (jobs, social and professional associations, diet and weight management, money management, and personal time management) have been directly influenced by my need to get things back "in balance" for me. Take the time (and have the courage) to honestly assess how your life is evolving relative to who you are as a person, and take any action needed to get (or keep) your life in balance for you.

Finally, be committed to being who you are. Many times, in life, you will be challenged to be something other than who you are. Someone or some circumstance may make you feel inadequate, or that your values or principles are wrong or out of fashion. You may get the sense that you're not good enough, smart enough, attractive enough, or worthy enough. As a consequence, you'll feel the pressure to change who you are. Now, there is nothing wrong with trying to make yourself the best you can be. However, the intent of making those improvements is that you are becoming a better you, and not trying to be someone else or something you're not. Rightly or wrongly, we're always challenged in life to uphold our beliefs, to maintain our values, to feel good about ourselves, and to fulfill our potential. These challenges can cause us to make compromises in our lives that ultimately cause us to be false to who we are. Resist these compromises as much as you can.

In sum, take the time to get to know you. It's hard to really like someone you don't know. The more you know and understand yourself, the more comfortable you will be with yourself and others. You'll be better equipped to make the decisions in life that are right for you and to find the kinds of friends and companions that will add joy to your life.

The Lord made you who you are for a reason, and there is only one of you. So, become an intimate friend with yourself, and be the wonderful person you were intended to be!

Love always,

Dad

FRIENDSHIP

He who walks with wise men becomes wise, but the companion of fools will suffer harm.

- Proverbs 13:20 and 17:17

Show me your friend and I will show you your character – African proverb
Hold a true friend with both hands

– African proverb

Dear Gaelyn and Erryn,

I think picking the right friends is one of the most important decisions you make in your life. The right friends will add tremendous joy, support and fulfillment to your life. Conversely, the wrong friends will bring strife, conflict, and even personal destruction. Few things say more about a person than with whom they choose to associate. So, I want to pass on a few perspectives on choosing friends.

First, let's define what a friend is. I separate friends from acquaintances. Acquaintances are people you generally know and have positive relationships with. Acquaintances can be professional associations or social associations. As I strongly advocate making an effort to be on good terms with everyone (to the degree that you don't compromise your values and principles), I think you should have many acquaintances. These are people you know and who generally know you. You like them, get along well with them, and enjoy their company. You may know some personal aspects about them (and have shared some yourself).

These are folks whom you'd be comfortable working with, traveling with, socializing with, and introducing to your family. However, do not confuse these associations with friends.

A friend is as precious a relationship as you can have. First, a friend is someone who has an intimate understanding of who you are, and you have the same knowledge about him or her. This knowledge is developed over time and built upon a trust foundation. This trust makes you both vulnerable to each other because you sincerely care about each other. It will enable you to confide in each other, sharing both pains and joys, good and bad times. It enables you to accept them, warts and all, and generate the same acceptance from them.

True friendship is not limited by the usual boundaries that govern other relationships. It is open, candid, supportive, forgiving, and long-term. True friends can disagree with each other and even get angry at each other. However, they seek to resolve issues instead of letting them fester. They don't let self-interest or self-centeredness get in the way. True friendship facilitates honesty because truth is used to help and heal. It is a bond created between people who sincerely care for each other, who will do their utmost to be supportive, and who respect and like each other so much that they would never do anything to intentionally hurt, embarrass, demean, or take advantage of each other. True friends bring out the best in each other because of the positivity they bring to this relationship.

There is mutuality and reciprocity.

This definition may sound utopian. I do admit that it's an ideal. However, I contend that it is this ideal that should be your yardstick in measuring the quality of your friendships. While I think you should have many good relationships, your friendships should be few. You'll not find many people who will measure up to these standards. That's OK. The key is finding the few who do.

Those are the ones to quote Shakespeare that you want to "bind to yourself with hoops of steel." So, give a lot of thought to whom you call your friend. Ensure that they qualify for that designation (and that you do for them as well). And don't be surprised if you find that you have only one or two, or if those friends you thought you had don't "measure up." True friends are rare; that's what makes them so valuable.

Love always,

Dad

EVERY DAY IS A NEW BEGINNING

Give us this day our daily bread.

- Matthew 6:10

However long the night, the dawn will break.

– African proverb

Dear Gaelyn and Erryn,

I'm sure you've heard the statement, "Today is the first day of the rest of your life." I truly believe that's true. Every day is a chance to begin again, regardless of what happened the day before.

As Erykah Badu indicates in her song "Bag Lady," carrying "baggage" does you no good. We all have "things" from our past that we tend to carry. Most often, it's negative things: hurts, disappointments, embarrassments, mistakes. These negative things tend to fester like an untreated wound, and before you realize it you become infected with residual symptoms: fear, worry, bitterness, depression, low self-esteem and helplessness. Then, these symptoms develop into bigger issues: loss of motivation, lack of self-worth, becoming a "difficult" person to get along with, physical or mental illnesses, and losing hope in life. Once you get to this stage, it's hard to recover, and the consequence is living an unhappy life and never fulfilling the potential we all were blessed with at birth.

The key to avoiding this downward spiral is leaving the past in the past. As Timon told Simba in The Lion King, you've got to put the past behind you. To me, accepting today as a fresh start is the first step in that process. What you do from this point on is what matters. If something went wrong that could be fixed, use today to fix it. If a hurtful situation from yesterday should be acknowledged and addressed, use today to do so. If there is a setback that happened, use today to determine how to deal with it or what the next step you can take. If there are things you can resolve, use today as the opportunity. Don't wallow in what should have happened, didn't happen, or shouldn't have happened that way. Acknowledge what did happen, but then move on.

To take advantage of today, you must be willing to move on. Notice I didn't say ignore the past. In all honesty, I really don't know if it's possible to forget something that truly upsets us totally. Whatever happened did happen, like it or not.

However, I absolutely believe it's possible (and necessary) not to let such instances linger with you, eat away at you, or weigh you down. You can let go of them, and you do so when you commit to moving on. Moving on requires that you take positive action. This action may be talking with someone to resolve an issue, or deciding what alternatives you have after a setback, and pursuing one of them. It may be acknowledging an error on your part and owning up to it, and addressing it. It may also involve having a heart-to-heart talk with yourself (or with someone close to you) about what you're not doing or what you should stop doing, and then defining a path of next steps to do the right thing.

You make the most of today when you use it to move your life forward, and it's hard to move forward when you let negative things hold you back. Regardless of what happens in your life, remember that today is God's gift to us to move forward and take positive action. As the saying goes, "that's why today is called the present."

Love always,

Dad

LOVE AND SEX

My beloved is mine, and I am his. I am my beloved's, and his desire is for me.

- Song of Solomon 2:16, 7:10

Tell me who you love, and I will tell you who you are.

– African proverb

Dear Gaelyn and Erryn,

I've wrestled with what I wanted to say to you here. I even thought about skipping this topic entirely. However, I would not be doing my job as your father if I avoided this subject, regardless of how uncomfortable it may be for me (or even for you). So, here goes.

Next to life, I believe love is the greatest gift God has given us. The Apostle Paul's treatise on love says it better than I'll ever be able to (1 Corinthians Chapters 1-13). To be in a loving relationship is the best experience one can have in life. Knowing that there is someone (or a group of people) who truly care for you and care about you, who accept you as you are and support you being all you can be, who feel your joys and pains as much as you do, who sincerely want the best for you and will give of themselves to provide their utmost for you, this is life at its best. A loving relationship doesn't require wealth or education, talent, or skills. It doesn't matter how old you are, or what you look like, or where you come from. All that matters is establishing a relationship in which you and another can appreciate each other as you truly are, and then allowing that appreciation to grow and mature to the point that you grow beyond friendship to becoming one with each other.

At this point, the two of you "complete" each other. The person you love becomes so much a part of you that you feel incomplete without that person. This person brings so much to your life that your voids are filled. Your loved one makes you a better person, gives you joy in just being with you, gives you hope and confidence, increases your self-esteem, and motivates you to realize your potential. Equally important, you do the same for your loved one, and this mutuality is the resource that keeps your relationship strong.

In this context, having an intimate physical relationship takes on a special meaning. You two literally give yourselves to each other, and the intensity of your emotional relationship gives this physical expression greater depth, passion and worth. This is what "making love" is all about: the physical expression of a deep and sincere emotional relationship. Making love is one of the most satisfying and fulfilling experiences that two people can have with each other. It is the ultimate expression of "oneness."

That being said, behavioral research has shown that the sex drive in humans is one of our strongest urges. And I'm sure you both realize that the relationship I described above is not the scenario for most people today engaged in sexual activity. Our society today seems to revel in the idea of casual or even recreational sex. There is no emphasis on the value of a relationship or the importance of knowing someone intimately before becoming physically involved with them. Consequently, having sex (or "hooking up" as it's called by your contemporaries) is now practically viewed as a "thing to do," a pursuit of pleasure, a transitory engagement in physical satisfaction with little (or no) emotional connection.

As maturing young women, I recognize that the urge for physical intimacy will occur with you as it has for anyone else your age. In addition, you'll be of interest to others who will desire to have that kind of engagement with you. So, you will have decisions to make. My hope and preference are that if and when you do so, you'll choose to make love versus just having sex.

That will mean being very selective on your choice of partner and, ideally, only becoming engaged with someone about whom you've given real consideration. The temptation will always be there to have sex, and while this may provide some temporary satisfaction, it will never provide the fulfillment experienced in making love.

Ideally, this should be your husband (or someone who could be your husband), reflecting the depth, quality, and sincerity of your relationship as partners in life. Ensure the person you give yourself to is truly worthy of your gift.

Finally, being your father, I'm obligated to remind you to protect yourselves. Don't engage in unprotected sex, even with someone you know well. Your life is too precious to us (and hopefully to you, too) to risk getting a sexually transmitted disease. If he cares about you, this should not be an issue. Also, protect yourself from an unwanted pregnancy. Don't let an hour of passion result in unplanned parenthood. I've rarely seen such situations work out well for the parents or the child. Last, when you decide to pursue a long-term relationship, mutually agree to have blood tests to confirm your health status before you increase your intimacy. You both owe this to each other as well as to yourselves.

Well, I made it through that part, and (presuming you've read this far) you have, too. If you've ever wondered how much I love you, let this letter be a reminder!

Love always,

Dad

MONEY

For where your treasure is, there will your heart be also.

– Matthew 6:21

Honor the Lord with your substance and with the first fruits of all your produce; then your barns will be filled with plenty and your vats will be bursting with wine.

– Proverbs 3:9-10

If you cannot have what you like, then like what you have.

– African proverb

Dear Gaelyn and Erryn,

Well, here is another fun topic to cover. Over the years, we've had lots of conversations about money. We've probably covered this more than any other single subject, in part because money tends to intersect with so many areas of our lives. It's almost impossible to talk about anything without money coming into it at some point.

I don't subscribe to the opinion that money is the "root of all evil." Money is neither bad nor good. It just "is," like any other thing made by man. It's your attitude toward money and how you choose to use it that is good or bad. So, I want to focus my comments on what your attitudes and uses should be concerning money.

First of all, money is a tool, a means to do something. It is not an end or destination. Money is not happiness, but can be used to obtain things that make you happy. It is not contentment, although it can be used to buy things that make you feel contented. Money is not a state of being. Instead, it is a resource that you can use to achieve the state you desire, or if misused, can relegate you to a state you'd prefer to avoid. So, please understand what money is and what it isn't, because it is this understanding that will enable you to keep money in its proper perspective and to use it appropriately.

Second, since money is a tool, the next consideration is how much you need. Don't say as much as I can get. There are many ways to get lots of money, but they all come with trade-offs. Prisons, courts, and cemeteries are full of people who wanted to get lots of money, but compromised their values, the law, and ultimately their lives. So, the pursuit of money is not the goal. The goal is to determine what needs and wants you have. What kind of life do you want to live? What experiences in life would you like to have? What will give your life meaning, value, and fulfillment? Like the points I made in the "Be True to You" Letter, you need to spend time assessing what you want your life to be. Only then will you be able to define the role money will play in your life. Money will be one of the tools or resources to help you live the life you want.

As a personal example, I spent a lot of time as a youth (right through college) imagining the life I wanted. I wanted to have a white-collar job (specifically, a lawyer), a nice house in the suburbs (like my aunt and uncle, the Sumpters), and a nice car to drive (a big 4-door sedan like the Buick Electra 225). I wanted a pretty, loving, intelligent wife and a family (ideally, two children). I wanted to live in a big city (New York specifically) and do the things I thought would be fun: dining out, going to concerts, sporting events, movies, and plays. I wanted to be well-dressed and groomed. And I wanted to be able to travel, particularly during the winter, to places that were warmer than Akron, Ohio! I had no idea how much it would cost to live this kind of life, but I knew this was what I wanted. That "life" became a major motivation for doing well in school, including graduating from college, to pursue this dream. I had a dream job (being a US Supreme Court Justice), and I set my salary target at what they were making at that time. That's what I thought I would need to earn to ultimately live the life I wanted. As you know, I didn't become a lawyer, but the career I eventually chose allowed me to achieve virtually everything I hoped for, and many things I had never imagined. So, set your target for what you want for your life first, and then determine what it will take for you to achieve it.

Third, fulfilling your dreams doesn't happen immediately. It takes time and commitment. Consequently, as you begin making money, your use of it needs to be proportional to how much of it you have. This leads to the most crucial concept about money: living within your means. Most people's wants exceed their means. That's not necessarily a bad thing in and of itself, because the desire to achieve our wants can be the positive motivation to work toward obtaining them. However, when people let their wants compel them to spend beyond their means, it becomes a bad thing. They get themselves into a quicksand of debt and financial problems that not only hurt their present situation, but also often ruin their future ability to achieve their dreams. This is the situation you absolutely must avoid. Developing the attitude of living within your means while pursuing your dreams is the most important lesson regarding money you can learn. Being able to do this is the foundation for keeping money in its proper perspective.

Fourth, the ability to live within your means requires learning to do three important things:

Establish a budget – Once an income is established, you need to manage it. The key to managing it is creating your personal or household budget. This budget can be made on an annual or monthly basis, although I prefer a monthly budget because it's easier to track with your monthly spending needs. The components of this budget should include: your basic living expenses (such as housing, food, utilities, telephone/internet connection, transportation, personal savings), your ancillary living expenses (things like clothing, household supplies, furnishings, insurance, debts, professional or family expenses) and your tertiary expenses (recreational or leisure activities, travel, hobbies, personal/home/professional services).

Your basic expenses are a must to cover. The ancillary expenses are things you have to cover, too, but these expenses will vary based upon your needs at any given time. That being said, the goal is to keep these as few as possible. The tertiary expenses are those that reflect more "wants" than needs. These are the ones you have to be most careful of and keep as few as possible. More often, it's poor management of the ancillary and tertiary expenses that wreck people's finances. So, build your budget to make sure that you cover your basic expenses first, and then see what you have available for ancillary expenses next, and tertiary expenses last.

Note that I included savings in the basic expenses. It is critical to good money management that you establish the habit of saving. Make this a monthly payment to yourself. Determine the amount you can afford to set aside consistently (e.g., 5% of your monthly take-home pay), and consistently put that amount into a savings account. If you're diligent and are able to save up a good amount, look to invest some of it in interest-bearing accounts, stocks, or bonds. This is your "rainy day" fund; the emergency money to cover unexpected needs or to eventually get something you can't afford right now. Your goal should be to get this fund equivalent to 6 months of your take-home pay. Make sure you contribute to your savings before you even consider your ancillary expenses, and well ahead of your tertiary expenses. In fact, if you do this properly you can really control these other expenses, as you'll have cash on hand without having to resort to incurring debt or over-spending.

In addition, when you start working, establish a 401K account (or a comparable investment account). Even if your employer doesn't offer one, start one for yourself (most banks or investment firms can do this for you). Ideally, the deposits for this account should come directly from your gross paycheck as a payroll deduction. The beauty of this account is that it is an automatic investment for the future. You determine how much you want to deposit into it, and with every paycheck, that amount is put into your account. You'll be amazed at how much you can save this way. And while it's meant to be a long-term investment account, you do have the flexibility of borrowing against it if you need the money for an emergency (but you will have to pay it back or you'll suffer a fairly stiff tax penalty).

Know the difference between an investment and an expense – One of the most improperly used phrases is: it's a good investment. This is typically applied to expensively priced items and is used to justify the relative cost of these items versus others that can provide the same benefit for less money. So, I want to clarify the difference between an investment and an expense. An investment increases in value over time; an expense does not. If you put $100 into a savings account that earns 2% interest annually, you'll have $102.50 at the end of the year. If you buy a pair of shoes for $100, they will never be worth more than when you bought them. Now, that's not to say that they aren't good shoes, or that they won't give you good utility and performance. But you may be able to find $50 shoes that can do the same thing as the $100 shoes without giving away an extra $50 that could be used elsewhere (or simply saved and invested).

My point is that you need to avoid spending more on things than is necessary. To be clear, I'm not saying that you should get the cheapest things you can find. My colleague and friend, Eduardo Correia, introduced me to this wonderful saying: "The cheap man always pays twice." First, he pays for what he got. Then, he pays again to either fix it or replace it when it fails to perform. I wholeheartedly agree with that. I believe you should always strive to get the best quality for your money. However, recognize that such purchases are expenses, not investments.

Therefore, you need to make sure that what you spend on "quality" fits within your budget. If the $50 shoes are well-made, fit comfortably, and look good, then they are a better expense than the $100 shoes with the designer label.

This idea is not limited to shoes or clothing, but to everything you buy. Whether it's shampoo and nail polish or automobiles and vacations, don't spend more than you need to. Also, take the time to prioritize what you feel is worth spending a little extra for and what isn't worth paying more for. There may be things that are important to you or necessary for your well-being (personal or professional) that warrant spending a little extra to ensure that you get what you want. However, make those the exceptions in your budget. The majority of your spending should be getting what you need at the least amount of expense as possible. If you do this, you'll find it much easier to manage your budget comfortably and avoid getting into financial difficulties.

Think cash versus credit – The biggest reason most people have money problems is that they overuse credit. They don't have the cash to pay for what they want (or need), and they have to rely on credit (loans, credit cards, installment payments with interest accounts). While there will be appropriate instances when purchases should be made with credit or loans (major purchases like buying a house or a car), the vast majority of your purchases should be made with cash. If you operate on a cash basis, you will be less likely to overspend. Your purchase will be governed by what you can really afford and you'll avoid building unnecessary debt. You'll do less impulse buying and more planned purchasing, because you'll need to manage your cash flow and savings to make sure that you have the money to get what you want.

The biggest challenge in doing this is controlling your wants. The desire to have things now is the key motivator for using credit. Developing the discipline to wait until you have the cash for something (or to forego it entirely if you can't afford it) is critically important to good personal financial management. As a society, we're encouraged to want immediate gratification. However, that will lead you to making poor money management decisions if you don't exert self-control. So, if you operate from the perspective of cash versus credit, you'll really help yourself in developing this discipline.

Finally, there is one commonality between money and love: both are meant to be shared with others. Don't let money make you selfish and greedy. Instead, be willing to share your wealth with organizations or services that take care of those less fortunate than you. Whether it's making a pledge to your church or finding a charity to support, use some of your money to promote good works. Whatever your feelings may be about your financial sufficiency, I can guarantee you that there are many others who are a lot worse off than you are. In fact, they'd trade places with you in the blink of an eye. Always view what you have as a blessing from God, and maintain the willingness to share that blessing with others in need. I have consistently found that being charitable begets additional blessings to the giver, sometimes financially and sometimes in other ways. Doing the right thing is never wrong, and I believe sharing with others less fortunate is the right thing to do. I trust that you will as well.

Well, I knew at the start this would be one of my longer letters, and hopefully you read it all the way through. I realize that there is a lot more to managing money than what I covered above, but I think these are the basics for good financial health. I must confess that I've learned most of these lessons the hard way, and I'm hopeful this letter will help you avoid my mistakes.

Love always,

Dad

BEING BLACK

It's not what you are called, but what you answer to.

– African proverb

Dear Gaelyn and Erryn,

While we've touched on this topic frequently over the years, I wanted to make sure that I addressed it one more time because I think it's still important. Despite being in the 21st century, race is still an issue in this country. While we appear to be on the verge of having our first African American major party nominee for US President, we are still a country struggling to find true racial and ethnic harmony.

As a child of the '60s, I saw the Civil Rights Movement first-hand. So, I know the efforts that have been made to progress our rights and freedoms to where they are today. Our collective status as a people in this country has improved significantly during my lifetime. However, this improvement has not been uniformly experienced across all segments of our African American population.

In fact, the dichotomies within our people are starker than they were when I was a child. On one side, we have the largest number of African Americans in the middle, upper-middle, and upper classes in this country than ever before in its history. Black people can be found in virtually any profession, living in affluent suburbs across the country, and in high-profile leadership positions in government and business. Simultaneously, we are still disproportionately represented in the bottom strata of this country, particularly in the areas of poverty, unemployment, teenage single-parents, high school dropouts, and the percentage of groups in prison.

While these disparities have existed within our people for decades, I believe they have become even more extreme. When I grew up, it was common for affluent Blacks to live near less affluent Blacks. While these groups had different financial statuses, they still went to the same churches, their kids usually attended the same public schools, and there was a common sense of identity. By contrast, these two groups today are not similarly engaged. Affluent Blacks will live in different neighborhoods from less affluent Blacks. Their children will attend different schools more often than not. They may not attend the same churches, social functions, or community organizations. The ultimate consequence of this is that we end up losing that common sense of identity.

These contrasts are most evident in the media. You have the superstar celebrities (who are presented as aspirational role models on one hand, and then a laundry list of various thugs and miscreants paraded through the local and national news. In between these two extremes, you have the "Hip-Hoppers/Rappers" who garner the same (if not more) celebrity status as the "role model" celebrities, while also glorifying (and frequently, participating in) the same nefarious behavior as the criminals covered in the news. Your generation has seen this latter group become the defining model of what it means to be Black today.

Now, I want to be clear about this: I'm not condemning "Hip-hopers" or rappers. While not a huge fan, you both know that I have enjoyed some hip-hop music and rap artists. However, I don't accept that they exclusively define what it means to be Black or an African American. Yes, it is part of our culture, but it's not the only aspect of who we are as a people. Being Black doesn't mean that you had to: grow up in a ghetto housing project, come from a broken home, be raised by a single mother with umpteen kids, resort to selling drugs or other criminal activity to survive, get arrested and serve time in jail, or become a young, unwed parent. Being Black is not just about speaking street slang, dressing in baggy clothes (or tight "ghetto booty" jeans), and having face tattoos. And it certainly is not about how light or dark your skin shade is, or the texture or length of your hair.

Being African American is about embracing the totality of our culture, recognizing and accepting it as an integral part of who you are. That culture isn't just hip-hop or a ghetto experience, but 400 years of struggle and triumph, pain and joy, repression and creative expression, and striving, surviving, and thriving. It's about knowing and appreciating our history, and understanding your responsibility to contribute positively to that history for future Black generations. It's about recognizing and embracing our contributions to American culture (and world culture), including music, art, dance, literature, fashion, sports, thought, science and social and political activism. It's about taking pride in your "negritude," our universal connection to Black people around the world (the African Diaspora).

Being Black is a conscious recognition that whether you're affluent or poor doesn't separate us as a people. It's about rejecting an "us versus them" attitude. You can be articulate and Black, well-educated and Black, well-dressed and Black, and gainfully (and legally) employed, and Black. You can be inarticulate and Black, uneducated and Black, poorly dressed and Black, and unemployed and Black. In any of these scenarios, all that is required is recognizing and embracing your connection to our rich and deep African American heritage. Do this, and you're as Black as you need to be.

Love always,

Dad

TAKE TIME TO REFLECT

Take heed to the path of your feet, then all your ways will be sure. The wisdom of the prudent man is to discern his way.

– Proverbs 4:26 and 14:8

Do not look where you fell, but where you slipped.

– African proverb

Dear Gaelyn and Erryn,

There's a saying that goes: "If you don't know where you're going, any road will get you there." In other words, if you're just aimlessly wandering through life with no intended purpose or goal, you'll end up going nowhere. I once heard Rev. Al Sharpton say that the hardest people for a minister to eulogize are those who live "unfulfilled lives." Those people just existed. They never attempted to do anything with their lives or to make a positive contribution to someone else's life.

As I've stated previously in my letters to you (and hopefully in person to you as well), I believe we have a responsibility to do as much as we can to use the talents and abilities with which God has blessed us. This doesn't mean that you need to be rich or famous. It just means that you have to strive to make the most out of what you have. If your desire is to be a dance teacher, be the best dance teacher you can be, employing all of the talent, knowledge and enthusiasm into your profession at every opportunity. If your interest is in writing, then learn how to be the best writer you can be, accepting the critiques and commentaries as constructive guidance to help you hone your skills and develop your voice. You don't have to be a media superstar to live a fulfilling life. I believe there are millions of "everyday people" doing just that: utilizing their talents, giving their best effort every day, and, by so doing, making a positive contribution to society.

In this regard, I think it is important to remember that since life is a journey, it's important to take a time-out periodically to check where you are. Are you really doing what you want to do? Are you enjoying your life? Is there a balance between your professional and personal lives? Are you heading in the direction you really want to go? Are your relationships positive and healthy? Are you happy with the person you're becoming? Are you managing your life well (spiritually, socially, professionally, financially, physically, and intellectually)?

From a personal observation standpoint, I've found it interesting how infrequently the vast majority of people don't take time to reflect on their current state in life. Admittedly, we live in an era where our lives seem to be constantly consumed with activity. We work hard, play hard, wake hard, and sleep hard. Multi-tasking has become our way of life, and each hour of the day has to be filled with some type of activity. As a consequence, I think we allow ourselves to get carried away by the flood of "busyness" in our lives, not really noticing or appreciating whether this current is taking us closer or further away from where we want to be. Even if you have a clear idea of what you want in life and are intensely focused on it, you can still easily end up someplace you didn't intend. This is like someone who is driving in his car full speed ahead to his destination, but oblivious to the road signs signaling detours or road construction. Ultimately, he ends up at a dead end or gets re-routed many miles away from where he intended to be.

I believe taking time to reflect helps avoid losing your way in life. It's like pulling your car into a rest area on the highway, checking your map, and making sure that you're really heading where you want to go. However, there is one requisite for getting the most out of these reflection sessions:

you have to be really honest with yourself. Besides time excuses, I think the real reason most people don't engage in reflective life assessments is that they're afraid of learning the truth about their lives. However, I feel the biblical admonishment ("...ye shall know the truth, and the truth shall set you free") is the right prescription. You can't make your life what it should be if you aren't honest with yourself about where it is right now. And, ignoring the realities in your life and how you feel about those realities will never lead to their positive resolution. There will be many times in your life when things will be going great for you, as well as times when you'll feel everything is wrong. That's why it's imperative for you to have these personal reflection sessions periodically and consistently.

Doing them when all is well is a great way to get positive reinforcement about what you're doing that's making your life happy. Give thought to all aspects of your life, so that you can see both where the source of your happiness is coming from and how it affects the other areas of your life. Conversely, when things aren't going well, do a similar assessment and identify where the problem really is and how it's impacting the rest of your life.

So, don't be afraid to pull the car over, check your map, and confirm that you're heading in the right direction. If all is right, then proceed with confidence. If something is wrong, then identify where you need to make a "legal U-turn" to get to your desired route. Also, if you're unsure, go ahead and ask someone knowledgeable and trustworthy for guidance. Being confused or doubtful in life is not the problem. Instead, it is staying that way when you can do things to give you the answers or assurance you need. Don't deny yourselves the opportunity to lead the happy and fulfilling lives you've been blessed to pursue!

Love always,

Dad

WORK TO LIVE, INSTEAD OF LIVING TO WORK

Commit your work to the Lord, and your plans will be established.

– Proverbs 16:3

Pray for what you need, but always work for what you want.

– African proverb

Dear Gaelyn and Erryn,

As you both are now either embarking on or exploring your desired professional careers, I want to share some thoughts with you regarding work.

When I was growing up, work was a very defined portion of my parents' lives. They were not in professional occupations, as you know. My dad was a postal clerk, and my mom had a variety of service jobs at our local hospitals (food service, maid service, patient transportation service). They went to work, did their jobs and then came home. They were rarely (if ever) involved in work-related matters after their shifts ended, or contacted about work issues during their off hours.

They didn't think about work when they took their vacation days, and they rarely talked about work-related matters (unless there was something juicy or controversial going on). Admittedly, my parents weren't in high-paying jobs, but I think this reality was true for most of the working middle-class folks in my neighborhood. Work was how folks made their income, but it wasn't how they lived their lives. To be clear, my parents and their contemporaries took their work seriously. They worked hard and earned their pay. But the nature of their jobs didn't require them to make work a bigger part of their lives than it needed to be.

Conversely, as you've seen from your mother and me, our work lives are not as neatly sectioned off from our personal lives. We'll go to our respective jobs during the day, spend extended hours in our offices, and then bring work home.

Sometimes, we work during the weekends. I check voicemails every day, and we've both taken our computers along on vacations to "keep things from piling up," or "to finish up a couple of matters," or to simply "stay in touch" with things at work. Individually, we both make more than our parents ever did, and collectively more than they ever dreamed. However, in many ways, work has been the focus of how we manage our daily lives. To that point, I believe Sharon and I have consciously and consistently endeavored to make sure we had time devoted to family activity, particularly during the weekend. In my humble opinion, I think we did a good job at that, and I think you two would agree. Nonetheless, it was a committed effort on our part to establish and preserve that time, frequently devoting more time to work during the week to make sure we could keep our weekends relatively free.

I believe that the difference in work/life balance between Sharon and me and our parents will be just as great for you two versus us. In today's society, your occupation is as much a part of you as your gender or ethnicity. Technology is already making it virtually impossible to leave work at the office. Already, there are a myriad of devices to keep people tethered to their work and constantly accessible 24/7 anywhere in the world. So, the ability to balance your work and personal lives will be even more challenging than it's been for your mother and me.

One of the common issues in the workplace today is work/life balance. Increasingly, employers are demanding more of their employees. People are being expected to "go the extra mile" to do what their jobs require, and typically, that additional effort comes at the expense of their personal lives. Consequently, single people seem to have no time to meet people (aside from co-workers) to build friendships and relationships, young couples virtually have to make appointments to see each other, and families with children at home live their lives by a schedule of activities and availabilities. These scenarios can build stress and dissatisfaction, adversely affecting relationships (if not preventing them) and leaving people tense, anxious, depressed, and burned out.

Now, to be clear, I'm not in any way suggesting that you two become "clock watchers" at work, just putting in your 8 hours and nothing more. The reality is that jobs today demand that you do what is needed regardless of the time required. For that reason, I believe it is important to do three things to make sure that your work and personal lives don't get out of whack.

1. **Do what you love and love what you do** – There is a saying, "the man who does what he loves for a living will never work a day in his life." I absolutely believe that is true. When you can make your living doing what you truly enjoy doing, you are willing to invest the time in it that is required. In fact, you'll do so happily and proactively because you like it so much. You'll be excited and thankful to go to work, and you'll give it your all every day. And while there will be times when work will encroach on your personal time, you'll be less resentful of those demands.

    Now, the risk in this scenario is that you can become a workaholic. You enjoy work so much that it becomes all-consuming, pushing personal life and relationships to secondary or tertiary status. This is where one needs to be vigilant. Using the "reflection sessions" noted in my previous letter is a helpful tool to identify when work is absorbing too much of your life.

2. **Remember that your job is what you do for a living, not who you are as a person** – It seems during my working life, people have increasingly become oriented to the idea of "you are what you do." Notice how frequently in being introduced to someone or engaging in casual conversation with a new acquaintance, one of the first 3 questions asked will deal with work (e.g., what do you do, where do you work, what company do you work for, what is your occupation?). People will make instant assessments of your education, income, social status, interpersonal likeability and desirability based on your response to that one subject. As a consequence, it's easily understandable how people can wrap themselves up in the perceived importance of what they do. It says a lot about them (or projects a lot more about them than what may be true).

I think this is one of the worst traps you can fall into. I've known successful managers who were afraid of retirement because they wouldn't have their job titles to define who they were. It's certainly OK to be proud of what you do or where you work, but it's not healthy to have it take on more significance than it deserves. Your value as a person is not a function of what you do, but who you are as a human being. The occupation or field of work you've chosen to support yourself financially is a means to an end, not the end itself. I believe that keeping this in mind is key to helping you balance your work and personal lives. Being a husband and father, a Christian, an African-American, college educated, and a mid-Westerner are far more reflective of who I am than being a marketing executive.

3. **Establish the boundaries for your personal life and strive to maintain them** – When Sharon and I were starting out in our first jobs in New York City, we got wrapped up in the consuming nature

of our work. We'd work late, go in early, stop by the office on weekends, and carve out slivers of time for ourselves in the evenings. It didn't take long for us to recognize that we weren't spending enough time with each other. So, we made an agreement. From the time we went to work on Monday to the time we came home from work on Friday, there would be no grief from each other for whatever time commitment the job required. However, from the time we came home on Friday to the time we went in on Monday, we protected that time for us (and family after you were born). We acknowledged that there might be times when we had to go in on a weekend or take work home, but those were exceptions. I can honestly say that after 30 years of marriage, we've been pretty true to that agreement. But it took a lot of effort. We were often at work longer during the week to make sure we could free up our weekends. We learned to manage our calendars (and our bosses) to keep that time protected. When exceptions occurred, it was recognized and accepted as such, and we went back to normal the following week.

My point here is that this didn't happen by accident. It was a conscious effort and commitment on our part. We made it happen. It wasn't always easy (or popular), but ultimately it was respected. We made sure that our work didn't suffer, but we equally made sure that our relationship didn't suffer. You just have to set some boundaries for your personal time. It won't just happen on its own.

In addition to the benefit of having more time to be with friends and family (or just enjoy life by yourself), making time for life away from work is key to avoiding job burnout and resentment. Giving yourself some time and space away from work not only helps to refresh yourself, but also gives you time to get a proper perspective on work issues or think creatively on job-related challenges. Many of my "ah-hah" moments came during the weekends when I wasn't thinking about work at all. Just freeing my conscious mind to do something else allowed my subconscious mind to do its work, finding alternatives or new ideas that I couldn't see previously because I was too close to the issues. As a former boss of mine once said, "Keeping your nose to the grindstone only means that eventually you won't have a nose."

Knowing that you both are passionate individuals, I've no doubt that you'll fully throw yourselves into your professional pursuits, and ideally into career areas that you'll truly enjoy. However, as you do so, be mindful of keeping work in its proper perspective. You'll have a much more balanced life, and you'll be able to enjoy your work even more.

Love always,

Dad

FIND A HOBBY

It is not work that kills, but worry.

– African proverb

None is richer than the one who has peace of mind.

– African proverb

Dear Gaelyn and Erryn,

This may seem like an odd topic to write about, but over the years, I've come to appreciate the value of having a hobby. I honestly believe it is one of the most beneficial ways to add joy, meaning, and value to your life. To be honest, I never would have felt this way 20 years or so ago. However, in the interim, I've experienced the multiple benefits of having a hobby, so I want to pass that appreciation on to you two.

First of all, what I'm defining as a hobby is a non-work-related activity in which you are passionately and seriously engaged. It doesn't matter what that activity is (providing that it's legal and doesn't intentionally hurt anyone else), as long as it's something that can absorb you. It should be something you look forward to doing whenever you get a chance, and it should provide you with great joy, stimulation (mental and/or physical), and satisfaction. Also, in my opinion, it should be something that has an end result to it, providing a feeling of accomplishment when you've done something with it. It should require your full attention when you're doing it, and even represent a challenge to achieve its end result. However, it should not be a source of frustration or discouragement. If it's not fun and enjoyable every time you do it, then find something else to do because that activity is not performing like a hobby should for you.

As you know, my hobby is golf. In fact, it really borders on an obsession. However, that is one of the reasons I love golf as my hobby so much. Despite having grown up around golf (my dad was similarly immersed in golf when I was a kid), I had no interest in playing golf myself until I was in my early 30s. In fact, Sharon has to get some of the credit (or blame, depending upon your perspective) for encouraging me to find an activity to get me from being a "couch potato" on the weekends. So, thanks to the combination of her insistence and Uncle Chris' father giving me his old golf clubs under the condition that I would learn to play, I got started. Now, it's one of the four priorities in my life, behind my faith, my family, and my career.

I never had any intention of golf becoming as much a part of my life as it has. It was honestly just meant to be something to get me off the sofa. But over the years, it has taken on far greater value and significance for me than I ever expected. Those benefits are not just exclusive to golf, but can be obtained in any hobby you choose. So, I'll list those benefits below.

1. **It gives you a mental (and potentially, physical) "vacation":** As my professional career progressed, I found it increasingly difficult to leave the office mentally. Whether at home in the evenings or on weekends, or even on vacation, I found that "work" just stayed on my mind. Usually, it was issues, problems, or challenges at work that would seem to constantly linger in my thoughts, following me like a shadow. Ironically, the more I mentally dwelt on these work situations, the more stressful they became. They got to be nagging and burdensome, and it became more difficult to deal with addressing or resolving them because their presence was so overwhelming.

   When I got into golf, I discovered an activity that demanded my full attention when I was involved in it. Whether I was playing a round or hitting balls at a driving range, it took so much mental focus from me that the work issues were literally pushed to the back of my mind. Getting that mental break gave me the opportunity to engage with those issues with a clearer head and better perspective than I had previously. To be honest, this astounded me! Consequently, golf became a refuge from a rough day at the office or whenever I had tough issues or situations to deal with. It wasn't a substitute for prayer or leaning on Sharon or other close friends, but an adjunct to them. Frequently, it was the buffer to give me the time and mental space to come to grips with my own feelings before I expressed them to anyone else.

This is what a good hobby can do for you. It gives you a resource to help you cope with the rough spots in life in a positive and personally productive way. Based on what I've witnessed from family, friends, and colleagues, hobbies offer a far better outlet than the options others often use (alcohol, drugs, affairs, and similar unhealthy behaviors). Aside from being a refuge or release, it helps you feel good in the process with no negative "side effects," ultimately putting you in a better position (and condition) to deal with the issues at hand.

2. **It gives you a sense of control:** As you know, my definition of stress is when you're trying to deal with something that is beyond your ability to control the outcome. You feel helpless and impotent, and that feeling has a tendency to bleed into other areas of your life. Under these circumstances, I've found that a hobby is a great vehicle to help you regain a sense of control.

    When you're involved in your hobby, you are doing something, and you are creating the end result. You are engaged in the process, and you are influencing its direction. This is why I believe a good hobby is one that has an outcome or resolution and provides a sense of accomplishment. When things are out of control in your life, you need to have something that is within your realm of influence, something that affirms your abilities and makes you feel good about what you can do. A hobby that lets you have those opportunities and experiences is a great resource during such times.

3. **It's a tension reliever:** In addition to helping, you regain a sense of control, a good hobby is a tension and stress reliever. It lets you throw yourself into it and release your emotions. Instead of taking your frustrations out on family members, friends, co-workers, or innocent "others," you can channel and focus those feelings into your hobby. There have been many a golf ball that's had someone's name or some situation transposed upon it as I was smacking it into space! In fact, a tough day at the office would often result in me visiting a driving range before I came home, just to make sure that I didn't have that tension walking with me into our house.

4. **It shows what you can do:** Another benefit of a hobby is that it reminds us of how good we are (or can be). When you have a hobby that lets you produce an end result, it gives you a great feeling of accomplishment. This reaffirms your abilities, talents and skills. It's tangible proof of your worthiness, enabling you to show to yourself (and others, if you care to share what you've done) your true capabilities. The universal sense of personal satisfaction for a job well done is as achievable with a hobby as it is with your work, sometimes even more so if you're the only one involved in your hobby. Again, this is best achieved with a hobby that produces an outcome or a visible end result.

Given these benefits, I hope you can appreciate why I place so much importance on this. In addition, these benefits should be a gauge to help you identify the right type of hobby for you. While golf is mine, reading and church youth activities are your mother's choice. Others like fishing, painting, tennis, gardening, writing, tinkering with cars, or working out. The important thing is to find something that's right for you and capable of providing the benefits noted above. It will be that extra "best friend" you'll really be glad to have.

Love always,

Dad

BE RESPONSIBLE AND TRUSTWORTHY

Let not loyalty and faithfulness forsake you...so you will find favor and good repute in the sight of God and man.

– Proverbs 3:3-4

There are two things over which you have complete dominion, authority, and control: your mind and your mouth.

– African proverb

Dear Gaelyn and Erryn,

My dad wasn't into giving a lot of advice or counsel. While he'd let me know if I did something wrong, he preferred to let me learn a lot of life's lessons on my own. However, one thing he did impress upon me was the importance of being responsible. He was big on that. "Do what you say you're going to do." "Don't make excuses." "Do what you know needs to be done." (That usually meant doing the dishes, cleaning my room, cutting the grass, and any other chores around the house before I was asked or told to do them.) Aside from saying it, he lived it. Every year of my adult life, I've come to appreciate more and more his dedication to being responsible for his family. Despite a relatively modest salary, he provided for my mom and me. All of our needs were met, and quite a few of our wants, even if he had to sacrifice his own interests to do so. He never complained or grumbled; he just did what he viewed as his duty to us. And while he was never a demonstrably affectionate person, he showed his love for us every day through his commitment to ensuring our well-being.

So, being responsible is close to being part of my DNA. I take it seriously, in part because of my upbringing, but also because it just makes sense.

Consequently, I would be irresponsible if I did not make this a focal message in this book. While I know this is a topic we've covered many times, I would not be my father's son if I didn't emphasize this subject in this book. (And let there be no misunderstanding, I am my father's son.)

If you take responsibility for yourself and what you can do, you are doing what is fundamentally necessary to live a healthy, happy, and fulfilling life. It is an affirmative way to live, because you're asserting ownership over the things in your life that you can control. Being responsible requires you to make decisions thoughtfully, be considerate in your actions, and treat others respectfully. It means you manage yourself with discipline, recognizing your moral and ethical values and using them as guideposts for your behavior. It shows you can be trusted and depended upon, and it sows the seeds for establishing a good reputation.

When you make mistakes or do something wrong (whether intentional or not), being responsible demands that you take ownership for your actions, deal with the consequences, and try to rectify any resulting harm.

My Dad equated being responsible with manhood, akin to the image Kipling projects in his poem "If". However, I believe it has more to do with being a mature person, regardless of gender or age. I've certainly seen some young people who showed more responsibility than adults (sometimes including their own parents). While there's no hard and fast point of demarcation, I think it's fair to expect anyone who's 16-18 years and older to act, behave, and live responsibly. By that age, one should have enough basic knowledge and understanding of right and wrong, good and bad, fair and unfair, appropriate and inappropriate to be able to live responsibly and to be held accountable for their decisions and actions.

Being responsible doesn't require wealth or formal education, and it doesn't matter what your ethnicity is or where you're from. It's something that anyone can do and, ideally, everyone should do. The world would be a significantly better place if everyone acted responsibly. While I accept that this ideal may be too much to expect, I do expect it from you. It is how you were raised and part of your familial heritage. As offspring of my gene pool, being responsible people and living responsible lives is your obligation to your ancestors as well as to your contemporaries and future progeny. And I trust that you will continue to conduct yourselves accordingly, as I'm proud of how well you've done so up to now.

Speaking of trust, I see responsibility and trustworthiness as being two sides of the same coin. If you are a responsible person, then you are someone I can trust. I have learned that finding people you can really trust is one of life's great challenges. By my nature, I am someone who is inclined to be trusting, but I've learned the hard way that trustworthiness cannot be presumed. I've discovered over the years that I can deal with people I don't like. I've even managed to work with people I didn't respect. But I've found it impossible to work or associate with someone I can't trust. Similarly, I've seen relationships repaired between people who disliked each other, and I've experienced people regaining their respectability, but I've never seen anyone fully recover from a breach of trust. It tends to be a stain that never gets fully removed.

So, in talking about responsibility, I have to emphasize the importance of being trustworthy. I think these are two of the most important qualities for building and maintaining a good reputation. I can't imagine anyone wanting to live with, work with or associate with someone who is irresponsible and can't be trusted.

Whatever faults or shortcomings you may have in life (and none of us are perfect), do all that you can to make sure that these two areas are not among them.

Let me close by saying that I am confident that being responsible and trustworthy are qualities firmly embedded in both of you. Your mother and I have seriously endeavored to make sure of that. However, it now needs to move from being our expectation of you to your expectation of yourselves. You will need to hold yourselves to these standards, making them as much a part of you as your gender and ethnicity. Beyond continuing to be good people, you will be doing your part to make this a better world.

Love always,

Dad

BE PREPARED TO COMPETE

Prove me, O Lord, and try me; test my heart and my mind.

– Psalms 26:2

Smooth seas do not make skillful sailors.

– African proverb

Dear Gaelyn and Erryn,

One of the many aspects of our family life I've really enjoyed is the time we've spent playing games. From board games to card games to word games to skill games to computer games, I got a big kick out of matching wits with you and watching your development as players. While my initial interest in participating in these family games was just to have fun with you, I quickly learned that these sessions were great vehicles to teach you both another important lesson: how to compete.

Like it or not, we live in a competitive society and, indeed, a competitive world. You've gotten a taste of that in your education process, striving to get good grades, make the dean's list, get into the schools you wanted, and get your diplomas or degrees. You received even more exposure to competing when you got involved in dance, gymnastics, and soccer. However, I was always concerned about how well those experiences helped prepare you for the competition you'd experience in the real world.

In the real world, the competitive environment is far more intense, and there are fewer support systems to help you do well. There is little concern for what happens to you if you don't "win," and not everyone plays fair or by the rules. In some cases, it's not even clear who you're competing against, what you're really competing for, and how the "winner" is determined. In the real world, there are no level playing fields and usually no referees. There's no scoreboard or tally sheet to let you know how well you're doing versus the expectation of your "judges" or the performance of your "competitors." More often than not, you won't have any "coaches" or advisors to guide, direct, or encourage you. Also, you will rarely have any "teammates" to rely upon.

I had to learn this lesson the hard way. Despite being a good student and playing organized sports in elementary and secondary schools, those experiences really didn't prepare me for the competitive environment in my first job out of college. Starting out as an account management trainee in a big-time New York City ad agency (Benton & Bowles, which later became DMB&B) was like diving into a pool of ice-cold water. It was a shock to my system.

You were given 18 months to prove yourself worthy of promotion to the next level (account executive, or AE). If you did, you got promoted. If you didn't, you were terminated. You were assigned to an account, and the AE was your direct supervisor. While the AEs were there to help develop you (in addition to the agency's excellent internal training program), they were primarily there to manage the account. So, if you required too much handholding or were developing too slowly, they were obligated to record that in your evaluation (which was done quarterly in your first year and semi-annually thereafter until promotion or dismissal). It didn't take many bad evaluations to get you shown to the door.

Needless to say, it was a rude awakening. And if that wasn't tough enough, I was learning to live in NYC, where you compete for everything (from getting a seat on the subway to buying a weekend movie ticket). Well, as you know, I survived, thanks in part to working for some great people (particularly Artie Selkowitz) and to a lesson from my days playing basketball at our neighborhood hoops court. It was this latter experience that I want to emphasize.

In my neighborhood, playing "pick-up" basketball games on our local outdoor basketball courts was the activity in the summer (and even during the decent weather months during the school year). The older guys (typically high school players or recent graduates) ruled the courts, serving as captains and picking the players they wanted on their teams. If you were good, you got picked. If you weren't, you had to sit and watch. If you got picked, but didn't play well, you'd be sitting out the next game. The games were tough, intense, and physical. There was no sympathy if you couldn't play or didn't get to play. You had to have "game" (or at least decent skills) to participate.

If you came by those courts in the evenings, you usually saw the younger guys practicing their shooting, passing, and dribbling skills. However, they weren't doing it to get good enough for the NBA, some college, or even the high school team. They wanted to get better so that they could get picked in tomorrow's neighborhood game. I was one of those kids, and with sufficient practice, I was able to get good enough to play in my share of games.

After a few weeks at B&B, I realized that I was back at my neighborhood basketball court. The captains this time were senior account managers, and they were picking their teams. They made assessments every day about who should or shouldn't be on their teams. Even though I had a job, I hadn't made the team. In addition, there were other trainees who had more "skills" than I did (MBAs, undergrad Business degrees, prior agency work experience). So, I had to work extra hard on my "game." I went to all of the training seminars and absorbed what they taught. I followed up with the seminar presenters (all of whom were senior managers at the agency) to ask questions on things I didn't understand. I used my current assignment to apply what I learned, in addition to doing the projects I was given. I studied the training materials they gave us in the evenings, and then I'd have follow-up discussions with my co-workers, bosses, and department managers to confirm what I had learned. The end result: I was promoted within the 18-month schedule and went on to have 3 additional promotions (including election to Vice President by the agency's management board) during my 9-year tenure there.

Again, I was blessed to have an excellent training program at that agency and some wonderful people who were willing to foster and promote my development. But none of that would have mattered if I hadn't realized I needed to compete and dedicated myself to improving my professional skills to be as good as (and in most cases, better than) my fellow trainees. Moreover, that realization has been a core principle in how I've managed my career ever since.

So, when we were playing our family games, it dawned on me that this was my opportunity to transfer my "neighborhood hoops" experience to you. Now, as you will recall, whenever we played a game, I never let you win. I never cheated to do so; I just played to win. If you wanted to win, you had to learn how to play better. And, you'd only win if you beat me fair and square. Cheating was never tolerated.

Well, it didn't take long for both of you to make beating me your number one objective whenever we played, and that was just what I wanted. You'd work harder every time we played to beat me. When you'd play just with each other or even with your mother, I knew that in the back of your mind, you were getting yourself ready to take me down the next time we played. And sure enough, both of you eventually got to the point where you could beat me on occasion and make every contest competitive. Believe it or not, I was actually happy when I lost to you, because in losing, I'd actually won. In turn, your victories were really more significant than you could appreciate at the time.

Now that you're grown women, your need to be able to compete effectively will be a key factor in your success in life. The further you progress in your professional career, the more intense the competition will be. You'll need to continually enhance and evolve your capabilities to maintain your desirability as a "pick" for your employer's team. Be mindful of this ongoing challenge and your responsibility to yourself (and any others who depend upon you) to keep your "game" sharp. You know how to compete and what it takes to win. However, if you ever need a refresher course, call me anytime for a game of "Scrabble."

Love always,

Dad

LEARN AND PRACTICE FORGIVENESS

As the Lord has forgiven you, so you also must forgive.

– Colossians 3:13

Forgiveness is a gift in itself.

– Bishop Desmond Tutu

Dear Gaelyn and Erryn,

In teaching us how to pray, Jesus indicates we should ask God to "forgive us our trespasses as we forgive those who trespass against us." I must admit that it took me a long time to fully appreciate the significance of that statement. As we seek forgiveness from God for our wrongs, we should equally forgive those who've done wrong to us. In fact, with Jesus' use of "as" in this statement, he implies that God should forgive us in like manner to how we forgive others. Now, as you know, I'm no biblical scholar, but I think Jesus's point in this statement is pretty clear: If we seek forgiveness, we must be willing to practice it.

Throughout your lives thus far, you've experienced your share of hurts and mistreatments from others (and sometimes, each other). Well, I'm sorry to say that such experiences are not limited to your childhood or teen years. In fact, as adults, you'll experience more hurts and disappointments than you have up to now. Some may come from professional associations (bosses, co-workers, subordinates), social associations (friends, casual acquaintances), and even family members. Most will be unintentional, but some will be deliberate. No matter how they occur, they will cause you pain, and this pain will be sharpest if the hurts come from those who are closest to you. Frequently, these are the people who know you best, whom you've "opened yourself" to, whom you've trusted or even loved.

When such occasions happen, it's natural to want to return the hurt. However, I want you to resist that inclination. Whether the hurt was intentional or not, taking an "eye for an eye" approach only leaves two people partially blinded. Revenge should not be mistaken for justice, regardless of what the wrong may be. Too often, a "tit for tat" attitude only leads to further escalation, heaping more wrongs on top of each other and creating a mountain of hurts that neither party can handle. There are a number of appropriate actions to take when you've been wronged, ranging from having a frank discussion with the person who offended you to engaging the appropriate authorities (including the police) if the matter warrants it.

My bigger interest in this regard, however, is how you deal with these pains internally. Do you let them nag at you, like a chronic headache? Do you let them smolder in the back of your mind, like a hot piece of charcoal just waiting to reignite? Do you pretend like it never happened and try to ignore it, like getting a stain on your favorite blouse and having to wear it the rest of the day? Or do you acknowledge the hurt and take positive steps to start the healing process, like you would with a cut on your finger (wash it, disinfect it, bandage it, and go on about your day)?

Knowing me as you do, I'm sure you know which approach I advocate (yes, it's the last one). When you're hurt emotionally or psychologically, I've come to believe you should address it the same way you would if you were hurt physically. You need to address the injury and get the healing process started as soon as possible, and I believe that forgiveness is central to getting the healing process underway.

Forgiveness doesn't mean that you agree with what was said or done, nor does it mean that you condone the behavior of the person who did it.

Forgiveness doesn't mean that you just accept what was done to you, nor that you shouldn't try to do something positive about it. Forgiveness is not a weak resignation to a wrong or a slight, nor is it a cowardly retreat to avoid confronting your injury.

The famous English poet, Alexander Pope, wrote: "To err is human; to forgive is divine." Indeed, practicing forgiveness is the elevation of our internal divinity to help us deal with life's pains and disappointments. Forgiveness is an affirmative step. It means you can separate the "act" from the "actor," rejecting the act and releasing any feeling of ill will to the actor. Forgiveness means you release the burden of the injury by releasing the negative feelings toward the one who injured you. Forgiveness frees you to move forward, breaking the tethers of the hurt that would otherwise hold you back.

I've seen through the years that people who won't forgive a situation from their past never seem to get beyond it. It's like a scab on a wound that gets picked at and, consequently, never heals and ultimately leaves an ugly scar. Their lack of forgiveness prevents them from being the person they could be. The irony is that the lack of forgiveness does little to the unforgiven. Instead, it just eats away at the person withholding their forgiveness. They become bitter and resentful. Or, they become guarded and cautious, never trusting anyone. Occasionally, they become "first aggressors," feeling that hurting someone else first will somehow protect them from being hurt. As a consequence, they just end up doing more damage to themselves than the original injury did.

Don't do this to yourselves. It takes too much effort to be a good person and do the right things in life, to let the weight of an unforgiving heart slow you down. I recognize that practicing forgiveness is not easy to do. In many ways, we're conditioned and encouraged to be vengeful. However, I believe we should resist this at all costs. Being forgiving is consistent with being true to our faith, practicing what we believe as well as what we hope to receive.

Finally, learning to forgive can best be started by forgiving ourselves. Often, we hold ourselves in contempt for things that we did or didn't do. Admitting our own wrongs and releasing the guilt and shame (including asking forgiveness of the ones we've harmed) is possibly the best way to start. Experiencing how it feels to forgive and be forgiven will give you the appreciation and encouragement to extend this relief to other areas of your life. If you're struggling with forgiving something or someone, pray about it and ask God for guidance on how to proceed. I've found that He will speak to you through the inner voice in your soul, and then you'll know the right thing to do.

Love always,

Dad

ENDING WHERE I BEGAN

So, every sound tree bears good fruit, but the bad tree bears evil fruit. Thus, you will know them by their fruits.

– Matthew 7:17, 20

When there is no enemy within, the enemies outside cannot hurt you.

– African proverb

Dear Gaelyn and Erryn,

I'm finally at the last chapter in this book. Hopefully, you've made it through all of the other chapters and digested the points I was trying to make. If some of it was redundant to what you've heard from me before, I'm relieved. At least I did convey some of these points to you in person, and hopefully at a time that was relevant and in a way that was meaningful.

It's taken me a lot longer to complete this than I had ever expected. The idea for this book came to me in the fall of 2001, and I began working on it at the start of 2002. Over the years, I've targeted completing it by your graduation dates or Christmas to give it to you as a commemorative gift for those occasions. But clearly that didn't happen, as you are both college graduates now, with one of you (Gaelyn) in graduate school and the other (Erryn) about to start her first job.

However, I consciously chose not to rush getting this done, because I wanted to make sure it said exactly what I wanted to tell you. I listed the table of contents first (in 2002), based on the topics I wanted to be sure to cover with you. But I decided to take my time writing each letter, waiting until my thoughts were clear on each subject. As of now, I've not re-read or edited anything I've written to date because I've wanted this to feel like one of our mealtimes or "family time" conversations. I'll have Sharon read this before you get it (she's a great editor and probably knows what I'm trying to say here better than I do), but I don't expect it to change too much.

So, as I wrap this up, I want to reiterate what I said in the first chapter, which is to know and always remember that I love you. You have both been a constant wellspring of joy to me from the confirmation of your embryonic existence. It has been a thrill watching you grow and develop into the wonderful women you are today. No father could be prouder of his children than I am of you. And that's not because of your scholastic or personal accomplishments, but because of the type of individuals I've seen you become. You have good heads and even better hearts. The world is a better place because you are here, and you will leave a lasting reminder of your goodness from the lives you touch and your individual efforts to be the best "you" that you can be.

While a product of your mother's and my DNA, you were formed by God to be the unique and distinctive people that you are. As your parents, and particularly for me as your father, our desire was to help you be the person God made you to be. We set clear and firm boundaries for your behavior early in your lives to make sure you were sufficiently grounded in good values and principles. But as you grew older, we gave you the opportunity to explore your own interests and make your own decisions. Sometimes that meant learning to deal with failures, setbacks, and the consequences of your choices. However, we were committed to always being there for you and helping you work through whatever challenges you encountered.

Now, you are at the point we endeavored to get you to: adult women whom we love and of whom we are extremely proud. Wherever your lives take you, we are confident that you will be successful, not just in the financial sense that our society likes to emphasize, but in the true sense of what our society (and world) needs. You'll be faith-centered, self-aware, and self-assured, productive, responsible, and meaningful contributors to our country and our world. You've been well nurtured, your wings are strong and you're prepared to fly. We look forward to watching you soar!

Love always,

Dad

ACKNOWLEDGEMENTS

I want to recognize the assistance of several people whose time, editorial comments, and encouragement significantly contributed to the completion of this book. First and foremost, I must give thanks and praise to God and my Lord and Savior, Jesus Christ. I do believe the idea to do this book was divinely inspired. While that statement is not to suggest that this book is a religious text in any way, I do believe I was divinely motivated to develop this idea and see it through to completion. So, thank you, Father, Son, and Holy Spirit! Amen.

Second, I want to acknowledge and thank my wife and the mother of my daughters, Sharon Walker, for her support and assistance in this book's development. From the initial idea, through the various rough drafts, she both appreciated what I was trying to say and provided great assistance in helping me communicate my thoughts clearly. Knowing my daughters as well as I, her insights were invaluable.

Third, I want to thank Odessa Whitaker Sumpter (my aunt and my daughters' great aunt) for her review and commentary of a later draft. A committed educator who is now in retirement, her keen eye and sound wisdom were invaluable in reviewing this text. As expected, Aunt Odessa provided wonderful support and suggestions, all of which I've included in the final version.

Fourth, I want to thank my dear friend Chris Nunes and his team at Cornerstone Strategic Branding for creating the graphic treatments for this book. Chris, your friendship and cooperation are sincerely appreciated!

Finally, I offer special thanks to Lawrence W. Young, my friend and fraternity brother, for his assessment, editorial comments, and creative suggestions. A retired educator and college administrator, and a close friend and trusted advisor since my undergraduate years, his input was particularly important in refining this book. Despite recovering from surgery, he gave full attention to this text and contributed greatly to its final evolution.

Biblical quotes were taken from the Revised Standard Version of the Holy Bible, a gift given to me by my grandmother, Jessie Rae Bellamy Whitaker. The African proverbs were obtained from a variety of Internet sources.

www.ingramcontent.com/pod-product-compliance
Lightning Source LLC
Chambersburg PA
CBHW031255120626
46545CB00007B/2832